SHIPS
In Plymouth Sound

HISTORIC PHOTOGRAPHS
FROM THE GOODMAN COLLECTION

Sydney Goodman

HALSGROVE

First published in Great Britain in 1999

British Library Cataloguing-in-Publication Data
A CIP record for this title is available from the British Library

ISBN 1 84114 026 0

THIS BOOK IS DEDICATED TO NICK BILSBY. HIS HELP AND
SUPPORT BROUGHT THIS PUBLICATION TO ITS CONCLUSION

HALSGROVE
PUBLISHING, MEDIA AND DISTRIBUTION

Halsgrove House
Lower Moor Way
Tiverton, Devon EX16 6SS
Tel: 01884 243242
Fax: 01884 243325

Printed and bound in Great Britain by Bookcraft Ltd, Midsomer Norton

CONTENTS

Plymouth Pier. An unusual view of the pier from Tinside, looking towards Rusty Anchor.

INTRODUCTION

For centuries Plymouth Sound has seen a wide variety of ships plying their trade, with many famous vessels associated with this historic anchorage. This publication covers the period from the 1890s, when photography became commonplace enough to provide a continuous historic record of the Sound, and continues to the present day.

The late 1890s and early 1900s saw the mail and liner trade increase, and this was to continue until the mid 1960s. Apart from the two World Wars, emmigrants, imigrants, mails and passengers continued their comings and goings from around the world.

Many of these shipping companies became household names, but sadly there are only a few of those well known names left today. Gradually they have all been absorbed into larger combines, or have gone out of business. Plymouth now only sees the occasional cruise ship, while traffic across the Atlantic has all but been replaced by the airliner. The transportation of immigrants and emmigrants has also long gone, and the only regular callers today are Brittany Ferries. These have built up a large volume of passenger and freight traffic to Santander and Roscoff, while Royal Fleet Auxiliaries and the small oil tankers and coasters continue to carry cargoes to and from Plymouth.

But let us go back to 1900, when shipping companies were building larger passenger liners and mail ships. At this time, as the volume of ships calling at Plymouth increased, so did the need for tenders to meet them, and trains to take the mails on to London and the North.

For many ships Plymouth was the first port of call and, by landing here for onward journey by train, passengers could save a day, while some mail could be delivered on the same day as it was landed. The Great Western Railway and the London & South Western Railway provided these services. The GWR purchased the *Cheshire;* passenger steamers including the *Antelope* and *Gazelle* were used as tenders and pleasure steamers, while the L&SWR had the *Atalanta* and *Victoria*.

The late 1890s saw the Hapag Line bring into service the *Augusta Victoria* and *Furst Bismarck,* whilst Norddeutscher Lloyd Line (NDL) introduced the *Kaiser Wilhelm Der Grosse* which, on her maiden voyage, broke the Atlantic crossing records both ways. White Star Lines were also regular callers. In 1900 Hapag's new liner the *Deutschland* started to call, along with the *Amerika* and *Kaiserin Auguste Victoria*, and the mail ships *Moltke* and *Blucher*. Around this time NDL took delivery of the *Kronprinz Wilhelm* which began to call, while the American Lines' *New York, Paris, St Louis* and *St Paul* were also regular callers.

While Millbay Docks was developed by the GWR for their tenders *Sir Francis Drake, Sir Walter Raleigh* and *Smeaton,* the L&SWR developed Ocean Quay for their tenders *Atalanta* and *Victoria.* Other tenders such as the *Cheshire* went out of service and, as traffic increased, the *Smeaton* and *Sir Francis Drake* were transferred to Fishguard, being replaced by the *Sir Richard Grenville* and others.

Many other shipping lines also called i.e. Leyland Line, Dominion Line, Cunard, Orient Line.

Hapag, NDL, American, White Star and NSAM were wholly owned or associated with the International Mercantile Marine Company, founded by J. Pierpont Morgan, the American financier, whose sole purpose was to gain control of the transatlantic traffic. Cunard moved their business to Fishguard and, in 1910, the GWR and L&SWR signed an agreement that saw the transfer of L&SWR traffic from Ocean Quay to the GWR at Millbay. The GWR purchased the *Atalanta* which was then placed on the Fishguard station, releasing the *Smeaton* and *Sir Francis Drake* to return to Plymouth.

At this time Southampton was making in-roads into liner traffic and White Star moved there, though re-instating their weekly eastbound call at Plymouth. They had also ordered new liners *Olympic* and *Titanic* which, on completion, would be the largest liners afloat. *Olympic* made her first call at Plymouth in June 1911, although history records that neither *Titanic* nor their sister ship *Brittanic,* was ever to call at Plymouth.

The Union Steamship Company and the Castle Line had amalgamated to form the Union Castle Line, their ships calling bi-monthly on the homeward leg of their journey. These were the *Durham Castle* and the ex-Union Line *Goorkha*. The Elder Dempster Company also called, and their vessel, the *Jebba,* ran aground near Bolt Tail on 18 March 1907 while bound for Plymouth. The Orient liners called every two weeks on the homeward journey from Australia; the Aberdeen Line called whilst outward bound for South Africa and Australia. P&O ships from Australia called fortnightly, and many ships of the New Zealand Shipping Company were registered in Plymouth. White Star liners such as the *Athenic*, *Corinthic* and *Persic* made outward and homeward bound calls.

The British and Burmese Steam Navigation Company ships made intermittent calls, and Booth Line vessels, from South America, were also callers. Many of these ships would soon be involved in the First World War, being used as Hospital ships, Armed Merchant Cruisers or Auxiliaries. A number were to be lost in action.

After the war ships of the NDL and Hapag were to be handed to the allies as war reparations, soon to be painted in the colours of their new owners and renamed. During the 1920s the number of passenger and mail ships calling at Plymouth doubled, and to meet these demands new facilities and two new tenders were ordered. These were the *Sir John Hawkins* and *Sir Richard Grenville*. The *Smeaton* and *Sir Richard Grenville*(1) were sold. This left four tenders, the *Sir Francis Drake*, *Sir Walter Raleigh*, *Sir John Hawkins* and the *Sir Richard Grenville*(2). These remained in service, apart from World War Two, until the older two vessels were disposed of.

After the war airliners began to make inroads into the liner traffic, and where it once took five days to cross the Atlantic, or six weeks to reach Australia, the airliners completed the trip in as many hours as the liners took days.

In the later half of the 1950s there were about two hundred calls by liners to Plymouth each year, but this was to drop further until, in the early 1960s, it had fallen to less than one hundred. The Immigration Bill of 1961, controlling the amount of immigrants entering the country, reduced liner traffic still further.

The end of Plymouth as a liner port came when the Compagnie Generale Transatlantique (CGT) announced its closure of the Plymouth call. At this time the company's new liner *France* was about to come into service and the *Liberte* was withdrawn, making her last call in November 1961.

Gradually the number of calls to Plymouth fell away though, in May 1962, due to a strike at Southampton, several lines diverted their ships to Plymouth. As air services increased so liner passenger services to many countries were withdrawn, the ships being sold or going to the breaker's yard. Late in 1963 the final liner called and Plymouth ceased to be a mail and passenger port.

The occasional cruise liner still calls but traffic today comes from coasters, fishing boats, pleasure craft and ships of the Royal Fleet Auxiliary, or those that have been chartered by the Admiralty, or foreign naval support vessels that may be visiting or training with the Royal Navy.

Yachting marinas flourish, filled with pleasure craft, while fishing vessels, thanks to the new facilities at Sutton Harbour, are much in evidence, and coasters, taking china clay to various ports in Europe and beyond, together make up the modern day traffic. Brittany Ferries traffic has increased on the Roscoff and Santander runs.

Tankers still deliver petroleum products to Cattedown Wharves and the odd coaster collects crushed stone from the Pomphlett Jetty in the River Plym.

The largest liner to anchor in Plymouth Sound in recent years was the *Queen Elizabeth II,* running up to the 50th anniversary of D-Day in May 1995.

ACKNOWLEDGEMENTS

Text in this publication has been kept to a minimum to allow the photographs to reveal the story of what Plymouth Sound was and will never be again. Photographs are from the Goodman Collection and are published by permission of the trustees.

Thanks are also due to Keith O'Malley, Nick Bilsby, John Smith, Tracy Hall, the *Western Morning News*, Denise Goodman, and S.P.R.O.(N). for their help in its preparation.

THE PHOTOGRAPHS

Sailing boats ride at their moorings off Plymouth Hoe c. 1900 while, on-shore, flags are flying from the Bandstand and Smeaton's Tower.

Trawlers anchored off the Hoe awaiting their sailing orders in June 1907.

Fishing trawlers in Sutton Pool c. 1930s. It is low tide and part of the fishing fleet have landed their catch and await the next day's fishing.

Trawler *P371* under the walls of the Citadel as it makes its way into Sutton Harbour to unload the day's catch.

CITY OF NEW YORK. The Inman Lines' *City of New York*, as built. She was later to be refitted after being sold. She lost one funnel and a mast in the refit.

SS NEW YORK. The American Lines' *New York* at Plymouth. Formerly named *City of New York* when owned by the Inman Lines (see page 13). Pictured here on 15 July 1903.

SS NEW YORK. Pictured here sailing from Plymouth after discharging mail and passengers.

SS ST LOUIS. Another American Line ship, the *St Louis*, seen here at anchor and about to discharge mail and passengers. Note the US Mail penant flying from the mainmast.

GROSSE KURFURST. NDL's intermediate transatlantic liner *Grosse Kurfurst* anchored in Cawsand Bay. Residents of Cawsand and nearby villages would often walk to Penlee Point from where they could hear the music of the ship's orchestra being played.

TRAINING BRIGS. Two old training brigs in Plymouth Sound off Drake's Island. These vessels were used to train young seaman.

An unidentified passenger steamship about to anchor in the
Sound c. 1900.

A variety of steam and sail at the mouth of the River Plym in 1906.

SIR WALTER RALEIGH. The GWR tender lies berthed alongside the Princess Pier in Millbay Docks, awaiting her next call of duty.

SIR RICHARD GRENVILLE. The GWR tender *Sir Richard Grenville* leaving Millbay Docks bound for the Sound to meet in incoming liner. Note the open bridge and helmsman.

Another view of *Sir Richard Grenville* as she prepares to go alongside an arrival in the Sound order to pick up mail and passengers.

SS DEUTSCHLAND. Mail being offloaded from the Hapag liner *Deutschland* and on to the tender *Cheshire*.

Following which the *Deutschland* is shown leaving Plymouth homeward bound.

SS KAISER WILHELM DER GROSSE. NDL's *Kaiser Wilhelm Der Grosse* in the Sound in June 1906 transferring mail to the GWR tender Cheshire. Passing across her bow is the Royal Naval Torpedo Boat destroyer HMS *Ferret*.

The *Kaiser Wilhelm Der Grosse* leaving Plymouth after passengers and mail have been disembarked.

Mail bags being loaded on to the tender *Smeaton* from the *Kaiser Wilhelm Der Grosse* 18 June 1906.

SS MORAVIAN. The *Moravian* of the Aberdeen Line, seen here at anchor on 9 April 1907.

SS KRONPRINZ WILHELM. NDLs *Kronprinz Wilhelm* in Plymouth Sound in June 1903, these six views of the ship show her at anchor, with passengers boarding the tender, and the vessel about to leave.

SS KRONPRINZESSIN CECILIE. NDL liner *Kronprinzessin Cecilie*, new in 1907, entering Plymouth after her Atlantic crossing.

SS KAISERIN AUGUSTA VICTORIA. Hapag's *Kaiserin Augusta Victoria* arriving at Plymouth after her eastbound Atlantic crossing on 27 July 1906. The stern view shows her large size. The tender *Cheshire* leaves a broad wake as she returns to Millbay docks with passengers and mail from the *Kaiserin Augusta Victoria* on 27 July 1908. The third picture shows the *Kaiserin Augusta Victoria* underway.

SS MOLTKE. One tender has left the Moltke with a second one soon to follow carrying mail back to Millbay Docks.

SS MILTIADES. Passengers disembarking from the Aberdeen Line *Miltiades* to the tender. The picture above shows *Miltiades* ready to sail after passengers and mails have been taken off.

SMEATON. Passengers from the *Persic* boarding the GWR tender *Smeaton* to complete their journey to Millbay Docks. Special trains will take them to London and the North.

SS LA PLATA. The Royal Mail Lines' steamship *La Plata* in Plymouth Sound, with a variety of vessels in attendance.

RM MAJESTIC. The *Majestic* arriving in the Sound on 30 April 1908 to land mail and passengers.

RMS CORINTHIC. The White Star Line *Corinthic* entering Plymouth Sound homeward bound from Australia, making a regular call. The mails and passengers have been taken off and the second picture shows the *Corinthic* as she makes ready to sail.

CHESHIRE. The GWR tender *Cheshire*, with Royal Mail officials aboard, prepares to leave to meet a liner in the Sound c. 1910.

SS SALAMIS. The Aberdeen Line *Salamis* in Plymouth Sound on her outward journey to South Africa and Australia. She is pictured here on 5 July 1906.

SS VICTORIA. Two views of the London & South Western Railways tender *Victoria* leaving Ocean Quay to meet an arrival in Plymouth Sound.

CHESHIRE. Two views of the GWR paddle tender *Cheshire*, one of the first tenders to be used at Millbay by the GWR. The pictures show her paddle boxes on the bow shot, and the broadside view as she moves into the Sound.

RM ATHENIC. The picture shows the *Athenic* on 30 August 1908 leaving the Sound. She served the Shaw Savil & Albion and White Star Lines on the joint New Zealand service.

RMS PERSIC. The *Persic* is seen here anchoring and at Anchor. She ran on the Australian service.

RMS PERSIC. Passengers crowd the decks of the *Persic* as the tender draws alongside to take off mails and passengers due to land at Plymouth.

SS GOTHIC. Two dramatic images of the *Gothic*. The top shows her entering the sound and the bottom shows her inside Mountbatten breakwater, aground after her cargo of wool from Australia had caught fire. She was deliberately grounded in shallow water in order to better extinguish the fire.

SS JEBBA. Whilst bound for Plymouth the *Jebba* ran aground in thick fog off Bolt Tail, Devon. A tug is in one of the pictures, standing off to render assistance. The *Jebba* was owned by the African Steamship Company and ran aground on 18 March 1907, only hours after a White Star liner, also bound for Plymouth, ran aground on the Maenheere Reef off the Lizard.

SS HILARY. Booth Lines *Hilary* in Plymouth, seen here after anchoring on arrival. The line maintained seasonal calls at Plymouth on their South American service.

SS ROTTERDAM. The Holland American Line *Rotterdam,* first called at Plymouth in 1910. She was laid up in 1916 due to submarine activities and resumed her calls at Plymouth in 1919.

SS RANCHI. P&O Liner *Ranchi* arriving in Plymouth Sound to be met by a tender.

SS INDIA. P&O Liner *India* about to anchor on arrival from Australia and Bombay.

SS INDIA. Mail, baggage and furniture being loaded aboard the tender from the *India*, a case of everything but the kitchen sink!

PRINCESS ROYAL. The pleasure paddle steamer *Princess Royal* crossing the Hoe foreshore, c.1920. She was owned by The Saltash, Three Towns & District Steamboat Company.

SS LA PLATA. A broadside view of the Royal Mail Line steamship *La Plata*.

SS ORMUZ. The Orient liner *Ormuz* in Plymouth Sound, on the homeward journey from Australia.

An unidentified paddle tug and training brigs at anchor in the Sound, early 1900s.

SS LADY WOLSELEY. The *Lady Wolseley* leaving the outer basin in Millbay Docks during one of her regular calls in September 1908.

SS SALTEES. The steamer *Saltees* leaving Millbay docks to continue her coastwise service.

SS KILLARNEY. The SS *Killarney*, another of the coastal passenger cargo ships that made regular calls to Plymouth. Seen here about to leave on 20 June 1908.

GWR STEAMERS. Pictured are two of the GWR steamers that visited Plymouth or were stationed there to help out the tenders, or carried out excursion trips to other westcountry seaside towns, including Fowey, Salcombe and Torquay. Pictured are the *Reindeer* and the *Antelope*. The *Antelope* about to leave Millbay docks appears to be fully booked for the excursion.

RMS OLYMPIC. Two views of the *Olympic*, *Titanic's* sister. She is shown in Cawsand Bay in 1912. Tenders coming alongside the *Olympic* to take off passengers and mail; the tender ahead is the *Sir Walter Raleigh*.

SS SAMARIA. The Cunard Line *Samaria* dressed overall in Plymouth Sound.

SS SOPHOCLES. The Aberdeen Line *Sophocles* awaiting the tender in Plymouth Sound.

RMS MAURETANIA. The Cunard Line *Mauretania* called at Plymouth many times. She went on the Fishguard run but when Southampton replaced Liverpool as Cunard's transatlantic terminal, calls on her Eastbound voyages continued at Plymouth.

S.S .WASHINGTON. The United States Line *Washington* entering Plymouth Sound after her transatlantic crossing on her way to Hamburg in May 1933. The second picture shows the *Washington* returning to Plymouth on 10 July 1946, after an absence of seven years with the United States Navy, during which time she was renamed *Mount Vernon*.

SS VEENDAM. NASMs transatlantic liner *Veendam* anchored after her Atlantic crossing on 16 May 1938.

MILFORD. The tanker *Milford* anchored in the Sound in 1930. Her draught markings appear to indicate she is empty.

RFA SLAVOL. The *Slavol* arrives home after going to the aid of the Commonwealth liner *Jervis Bay*, on which vessel eight stowaways had mutinied and threatened to set the ship on fire.

NIEUW AMSTERDAM. The *Nieuw Amsterdam* arrives at Plymouth on 27 May 1938 on her return maiden voyage from New York.

FRA PRESTOL. The Fleet Auxiliary *Prestol* in the Sound, before moving up the Hamoaze to Devonport.

MV TARAKAN. The Dutch liner *Tarakan* at anchor in the Sound in 1936, with an attendant barge alongside.

ST CYRUS. The navy tug *St Cyrus* leaving Plymouth en route to Gibraltar. On her return to Plymouth she had on board survivors of sister ship *St Jenny* which had foundered in a severe gale.

RMS QUEEN MARY. Pictured here racing up the English Channel in 1936.

SS BREMEN. The record breaker *Bremen* arrives in Plymouth Sound in July 1929. She was awarded to France in war reparations after the Second World War.

SS LEVIATHAN. Formerley the German *Vaterland* after the end of World War One she was handed to the United States Shipping Board who, after using her as a troop transport, then handed her to the United States Shipping Line. She is seen here at Plymouth on 2 May 1932.

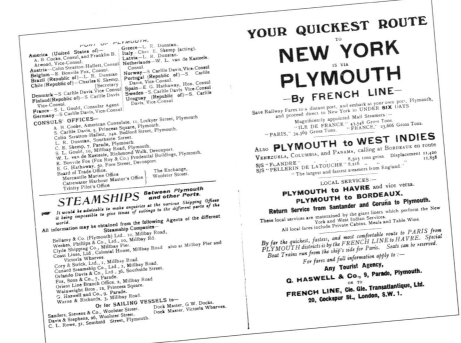

Top: SS BEACHEY. The Clyde Shipping Company's steamer *Beachey* on the Glasgow–Belfast–Plymouth–London run, leaving Millbay in October 1937.

Right: SS GOODWIN. The Clyde Shipping Company's *Goodwin* at Plymouth in September 1927. She was later sold and became the *City of Cork*. As the *Goodwin* she served as a Q ship in World War One.

Bottom: ORION. The Orient Line *Orion*, seen here in the Sound on 21 January 1936. She was to become a familiar and much loved ship.

THE NORMANDIE. These photographs sadden the heart. That such a beautiful ship as the *Normandie* should have a disastrous end, is a tragedy. On the outbreak of the Second World War she was trapped in New York and was taken over by the United States Maritime Commission and renamed *Lafayette*. In February 1942, whilst undergoing conversion to a troopship, she caught fire and the volume of water played onto her caused her to capsize. She was later raised and towed to a new berth to await her fate. This in the end was to be the breaker's yard, where she was taken in 1946.

RFA BACCHUS. The store ship *Bacchus* arrives in the Sound, the crew on board awaiting tugs to take her to her berth.

STEAM TRAWLERS. The crews of two steam trawlers going about their tasks whilst alongside the fish quay in Sutton Harbour.

S.S. VASSOS. The coaster *Vassos* aground in Sutton Harbour. She is carrying a load of potatoes to be unloaded at North Quay.

SAILING FISHING VESSELS. Pictured here in the River Plym at low water they await the new tide to resume fishing. Meantime the chance to paint the *Emm's* bottom is taken.

MB WILLOWTIT. The former french fishing vessel taken over in July 1940 and renamed *Willowtit*. Seen here in the Sound in 1942, she was handed back to the French in October 1945.

PRINCE CHARLES. The former cross channel ferry *Prince Charles* in Plymouth Sound. She had been taken over by the Royal Navy for use as an auxiliary.

HMT LORD INCHCAPE. Seen here in Jennycliff Bay in 1943. A fishing vessel taken over by the Royal Navy in 1939, she was sunk by a mine off Plymouth in October 1940, later raised and returned to service.

FISHING BOATS. Fishing boats, home from the sea. Their catches unloaded, the crews go about the duties of tidying up before they sail again.

RFA BISHOPDALE. A tug shepherds the *Bishopdale* into Plymouth Sound. Fully laden, she is making for the open sea.

SALVONIA. The salvage tug *Salvonia* in the Sound on 16 July 1946. Her normal station was Falmouth as an emergency tug.

SS OCEAN WAYFARER. Cargo ship *Ocean Wayfarer* unloads wheat at the Millbay silo. Behind the silo is the Queen's Harbourmasters Office Longroom.

SS ST JAN. The Swedish cargo ship *St Jan* unloads wheat at the grain silo in Millbay docks, the berth is now the Brittany Ferry terminal.

SUTTON HARBOUR. A scene vastly changed, the coal wharf has gone as have many of the buildings in the backround. Centre left can just be seen the City of Plymouth Fire Brigade fire boat/tender.

SS LIBERTE. The former German liner *Europa*, she was handed to the French as a war reparation, refitted and renamed *Liberte*. She is pictured here from the tender, just leaving her. Though larger than the *Isle de France* she was never held in the same esteem.

SS ISLE de FRANCE. Shown here after the Second World War, when she underwent a refit and lost one of her funnels. Of all the liners that visited Plymouth Sound she was the favourite of the people of Plymouth.

TS ARGENTINA. The troopship *Argentina* seen arriving in Plymouth Sound in September 1945. She had sailed up the Channel with all lights blazing - a sign that all wartime danger was now past.

HMS VULCAN. This photograph had to be included as she spent many years moored off Torpoint as one of the old ships that formed HMS *Defiance*, the torpedo training school. She is seen here under tow bound for the breaker's yard in December 1955.

WEST INDIAN ARRIVALS. Immigrants from the West Indies arrive at Millbay Docks after landing from the tender, and about to board the train for London.

TCV SWITHA. The tank cleaning vessel makes her way through the Sound bound for her next duty.

RFA ARNDALE. The *Arndale,* with the assistance of a tug, moves across the Hoe foreshore bound for the Hamoaze to unload her cargo of oil.

SS MORETON BAY. An unsual visitor to Plymouth the *Moreton Bay* about to enter Plymouth Sound after being diverted from Southampton due to a dockers' strike.

RFA BEDENHAM. The naval stores vessel *Bedenham* moving into the Sound having unloaded her stores. In April 1951, whilst at Gibraltar, she blew up.

SS RANGITATA. The New Zealand Shipping Company's *Rangitata* calls before sailing to New Zealand. Many of this company's ships were registered in Plymouth.

ST PATRICK. The GWR *St Patrick* seen here at Millbay Docks en route to Weymouth in June 1948 where she was to replace the former *St Patrick*, lost during the Second World War on the Weymouth–Channel Island run.

MV VENUS. A regular caller to Plymouth on the Bergen Line run to Madiera. She is pictured here aground in Jennycliff Bay after dragging her anchor during a severe gale, and after entering Millbay Docks before being taken to Devonport Dockyard for repairs.

MV METEOR. The Norwegian liner *Meteor* on arrival at Plymouth on 15 May 1959. She was on a cruise of the British Isles.

MV SAGAFJORD. The date is 9 May 1966 and the Norwegian liner *Sagafjord* visits Plymouth. Her ships' boats are taking passengers ashore.

MV OSLOFJORD. The Norwegian liner *Oslofjord* entering Plymouth Sound during trials off the South Coast in October 1949.

LA DUCHESSE DE NORMANDIE. This former GWR tender at Plymouth was sold when liners stopped calling. The first picture shows her berthed in the Millbay inner basin. The second shows her in Willoughby's dry dock, now filled in and providing the car park for Brittany Ferries.

MV REINA del MAR. The cruise liner *Reina del Mar* at anchor off Cawsand Bay in Plymouth Sound with a tender alongside. These two pictures show her anchored and just about to anchor.

WDV ST MARTIN. A familiar sight for many years as it passed in and out of Plymouth Sound, the *St Martin* is seen here in 1958. She was used for dredging Admiralty berths in Plymouth and other local ports.

RFA RESURGANT. A familiar sight in Plymouth Sound for many years, she is seen here with mist-shrouded Staddon wall behind.

MV ENGLAND. The *England* passing through the Sound to Devonport Dockyard where she was to load Royal Marines bound for exercises in Norway.

RFA EASEDALE. Another tanker, seen here after the war, had ended in black and grey livery. Today RFA ships are painted all grey. Note the gun sponson still in situ on her bows.

RFA BIRCHOL. A small RFA tanker that for many years was regularly in and out of the Sound as she distributed her cargoes to other ports.

MV CAERNARVONBROOK. One of Comben Longstaffs fleet of coasters that were regular callers to Sutton Pool coal wharf to unload coal. Other colliers like the *Richmond* and *Windsor Queens* ensured Plymouth's coal supply.

MV TANKERMAN. One of the many small tankers that call at Plymouth to deliver petroleum products to Cattedown Wharves.

LAWRENCE D. TYSON. The *Lawrence D. Tyson* in ballast anchored in Plymouth Sound awaiting orders.

MALCOM MILLER. The Sail Training Association's schoooner *Malcolm Miller* leaving Plymouth Sound.

PLUMGARTH. For many years Reynolds of Torpoint was the local tug boat company but they were taken over by Corys Towage, and *Plumgarth,* seen here with a barge alongside, was one of the new tugs that replaced the old steam tugs of Reynolds.

HMT SUPERMAN. Two views of the admiralty tug *Superman* in Jennycliff Bay with her charge about to swing the compass.

SPANISH SAIL TRAINING SHIP JUAN SEBASTIAN De
ELCANO. Two views of the Spanish Navy's sail training vessel
Juan Sebastian De Elcano passing Drake's Island as she moves
up river to berth at Devonport Dockyard in 1980.

ITALIAN SAIL TRAINING SHIP AMERIGO VESPUCCI. The *Amerigo Vespucci* has visited Plymouth many times. On this visit the author was privileged to board her off the breakweater and sail into Millbay Docks with her on her visit to Plymouth.

SAIL TRAINING SHIP DANMARK. The sail training ship *Danmark* entering Millbay Docks on 11 September 1980.

POLISH SAIL TRAINER FREDERIC CHOPIN. The Polish sail training ship *Frederic Chopin* anchored inside Mountbatten breakwater with Batten Tower behind her.

ANTONY. One of a numerous number of steam tugs owned by the Reynolds Company of Torpoint. She is seen here at her moorings off Torpoint. She and other tugs of the company provided towage in Plymouth Sound, the Plym and the Tamar.

MV POSEIDON. A visitor to Plymouth in May 1973, the *Poseidon* is seen here berthed in Milllbay Docks.

RMAS ALSATIAN. One of the many naval tugs that operated in the naval base and Plymouth Sound.

RFA FORT LANGLEY. Taken over by the Royal Fleet Auxiliary after the end of the war *Fort Langley* and many of her sisters became familiar sights anchored off the breakwater fort in Plymouth Sound.

RDV CRYSTAL. Built at Devonport Dockyard the research development vessel *Crystal* makes her way into Plymouth Sound en route for Portland Harbour in December 1971.

MV BRITISH DART. The tanker *British Dart* makes her way to Devonport Dockyard, she was chartered by the Admiralty during the Falklands crisis.

RFA FORT GRANGE. The *Fort Grange* is seen here with the breawater behind her as she swings at a buoy in the Sound.

BRITTANY FERRIES. Over the years countless thousands of holidaymakers have set off the for Continent via Millbay on one of several of the Brittany Ferries serving Plymouth. The top photograph shows *Cournalais* just reversed out of the Millbay terminal before heading into the Sound on her way to Roscoff. The middle photograph shows the *Quiberon* making her way to Roscoff, passing a power boat race being held in Plymouth Sound, in September 1983. The bottom photograph shows the Santander ferry *Val de Loire* in the Millbay terminal taking on passengers and their vehicles for the twenty-four-hour crossing.

RMAS PINTAIL. The *Pintail* for many years was a familiar sight in Plymouth Sound and other South West ports laying or renewing buoys, or on salvage work. She has since been sold.

NAV THROSK. The Naval Armaments Vessel *Throsk* leaving the Sound after delivering her cargo to the Naval Base.

RFA OLMEDA. The *Olmeda* is being shepherded downriver into the Sound in October 1982, either to anchor in the Sound or sail to another port or country.

FV ADMIRAL BLAKE. The Interfish Company trawler *Admiral Blake,* in Plymouth Sound. She and a sister ship are brand new and dressed overall for the camera.

RFA SIR GALAHAD. This picture will evoke many memories as it is the last one taken of her as she leaves Plymouth bound for the Falkland Islands where she was to be lost in tragic circumstances during the crisis.

RMAS ST MARGARETS. A veteran says farewell as she crosses the Sound with her paying off pennant flying after more than forty years service.

THE NESS SISTERS. Two of a class of three sister ships are shown here, the *Lyness* and the *Stromness*. The third sister was the *Tabartness*. All three were to be sold to the United States Navy by the Ministry of Defence.

RFA RELIANT. Pictured here the *Reliant* is loaded with vehicles and equipment bound for the Falkland Islands.

HMS NORTHELLA. A former fishing vessel, chartered by the Royal Navy during the Falklands crisis and retained as a navigational training ship until 1998. *Northella* is seen here being moved in the River Tamar.

MV ATLANTIC CAUSEWAY. After conversion and loading at the naval base she is shepherded into the Sound, bound for the Falkland Islands in May 1982.

HNLMS POOLSTER. A Netherlands naval support ship, *Poolster*, visited Plymouth on many occasions.

RFA BAYLEAF. The RFA tanker *Bayleaf* pictured here returning to Devonport after service in the Falkland Islands.

RMAS NEWTON. Seen here moving upriver from Plymouth Sound the *Newton* carries out a variety of tasks for the Royal Navy and Royal Maritime Auxiliary Service.

RUSSIAN SAIL TRAINING SHIP SEDOV. The Russian sail training ship *Sedov* anchored off Plymouth Hoe in 1997, making ready to sail. She returned later in the year for Plymouth Navy Days.

RMS QUEEN ELIZABETH II. Cunard's flagship arriving in Plymouth Sound during the 50th Anniversary celebrations of D-Day, on 8 May 1995.

JAMES CLARK ROSS. The Antarctic survey ship *James Clark Ross* about to berth in Plymouth during one of her rare visits. This view was taken on 29 March 1996.

RFA FORT GEORGE. A recent addition to the RFA Fleet seen here moving into the Sound ready to sail on 4 May 1998.

HMY BRITANNIA. The Royal Yacht *Britannia* moored off Plymouth Hoe. No longer in service she is now berthed as a static exhibit at Leith, Scotland.